in a bottle of ink

haiku - tanka - haibun

melinda b hipple

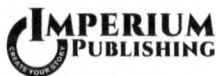

IMPERIUM PUBLISHING

first publication credits

haiku:
"the basket" – *Linx*; 2007
"making change," "lightning strike," "unexplored path," "column of smoke" – *Notes from the Gean*, June 2009;
"lingering light," "one moment ago," "the moon" – *Blogging Along Tobacco Road*, November 2009;
"summer clouds," "a tunnel" – *Notes from the Gean*, December 2009;
"hedgerow" – *Haijinx*, 2010;
"the little spider," "a spider," "lamplight" – *Tinywords*, 2010, 2011;
"threshold" – *Pirene's Fountain*, April, 2011;
"grandpa's jokes," "oscillating fan," "dad's funeral" – *Failed Haiku*, May 2016

tanka:
"a fly" – *Notes from the Gean*, June 2009;
"wrapped" – *Pirene's Fountain*, April, 2011;
"as are moths" – *Watershed*, 2014

haibun:
"Letting Go" – *Haibun Today*, 2011
"For Gene" – *Failed Haiku*, May 2016

(IMPERIUM PUBLISHING

1097 N. 400th Rd
Baldwin City, KS, 66006
www.imperiumpublishing.com

in a bottle of ink

these poems are written
in the Japanese tradition
of link and shift, and not
the western practice
of counting syllables

SPRING

making change
a dogwood blossom
on the counter

the chirp
of a car lock
spring rain

purple crocus
a complementary color
flies by

tip of a leaf
an inchworm stretches
into the sky

lamplight . . .
through the walls
the faint sound of geese

cloudburst
the shriek of ballerinas
leaving class

garden wedding
a butterfly opens
for the pianist

sapling
roots deeper
than mine

SUMMER

summer clouds
a dark strand divides
into geese

summer wheat
a bird cloud
thickens in blue air

summer breeze
the wind generators
in unison

prairie wind
the silver underside
of trees

overcast sky
sunflowers facing
in all directions

old pond
the sky folds in
to a striker's wake

midstream—
a damselfly
on my knee

skipping stone . . .
the many places
it will touch

river path
generations courting
the same fish

grandpa's jokes
the carp and I
take the bait

tinge of blue
the morning song of birds
after rain

wading
the dimples
in her cheeks

a subtle reminder
to share the sidewalk—
spider's thread

repair shop
a spider's web
across the fender

the little spider
hunches sideways
night shift

a spider
on the floor tile
checkmate

roommate . . .
making sure I know
where the spider is

silverfish
a ripple down
my back

a wasp
spiraling down the toilet
my apology

lingering light
a wasp barely visible
against the sky

last call
the drone of cicadas
on the walk home

between each
drip of the faucet
the buzz of a fly

coat pocket
a train of sugar ants
finds the mint

earthworm
in the ladies' room
gender confusion

piano practice
the syncopated rhythm
of a cricket

tree shadows
climb the brick wall
with the ivy

swayback horse
I twist a little
in the car seat

moon halo
horses nuzzle
in the field

a touch-me-not
face down on the pavement
mid-summer haze

AUTUMN

no room
for a hood ornament
luna moth

full moon
the celadon curve
of a moth wing

lost
a moth and the moon
inside my car

Venus
at the window again
sleepless in Kansas

autumn dusk . . .
cricket chirps
one at a time

autumn sky
a mosquito buzzes
the day moon

one moment ago
this light that touched
the moon

a path
for my thoughts
moon glow

computer solitaire
the man in the moon
over my shoulder

the moon
a little less than full
hope chest

threshold of
the last house we'll share
new moon

shattered glass
a web
of moonlight

post election . . .
an eddy of dried leaves
in the far right corner

hedgerow
the day moon and I
on opposite sides

heirloom
she works the needle
into autumn

cold drizzle
photos of my family
miles away

tucked into
the dove's folded wing
a new silence
                (for Deeva)

Diwali . . .
I light a chai candle
for one who can't

WINTER

mammogram appointment
a cluster of sparrows
in the bare oak

long winter night
the heat duct
ticking

grandmother's brooch
we add another date
to the family tree

my lip
frozen on the window sill
mother's voice

death watch . . .
he plays with the buttons
on his bed

the nurse asks
if we want pillows
long night moon

a stranger
in the casket
dad's funeral

sorting
dad's things—
microburst

steady rain
a widow's wail
above the hymn

state cemetery
each stone marks
a nobody

NO KIGO

wind chimes
inside the mini-van . . .
winding road

oscillating fan
this way and that
a dust bunny

navigation lights
too close for comfort
Mars blinks

pre-dawn
a satellite
connects the dots

unexplored path
a contrail through the heart
of the sun

deposits left
by morning dew
old voices

linen napkins
stories weave
in midair

the story
told in whispers
heirloom shotgun

memory foam
another anniversary
forgotten

lamplight
my shadow softens
with each step

the force
of each wave ...
blood moon

harvest moon
I skip
the tampon aisle

DNA test
the father she knew and
the father she didn't

Facebook channeling
six million ghosts—
Anne Frank's smile

the sky today
another Rorschach test

interstate—
we race
the contrail

lightning strike—
the earth shakes loose
a car alarm

the computer
reboots
a flash
of lightning

column of smoke
my neighbor's house
fills the sky

the edge of sleep
my neighbor lights
a fuse

sunbeams
in each room the same work
undone

bruise
where in the day's work
was there time for pain?

shaving my legs
for the first time in a year
new romance

pain in my side
medical tests reveal
a pain in my side

art lesson
kindergarten students
stick to the assignment

life drawing
the artist picks
his nose

tsunami
wave after wave
of news reports

exchange student
the same interpretation
of our laughter

a tunnel
through the mountain
swallowing my fear

Kansas
pole after pole
after pole

roadside ditch
headlights illuminate
deer in the queue

headstone
bees pollinate
the plastic mums

climate change
fueling the fires that fuel
climate change

all eyes
on the tractor
opening bid

broken conversation
curls of cigarette smoke
tethered to the bar

his cigarette
balanced on a matchbook
last call

tab receipts . . .
I borrow the barkeep's pen
to write haiku

last call
the first sound of rain
in weeks

PANDEMIC SENRYU

social distancing
I let others take on
the internet troll

COVID19
even my shadow
keeps its distance

spring in quarantine . . .
from my window I glimpse
the sprouting grass moon

quarantine day ten
my sixty-five-year-old
robot fan voice

a push
to reopen the economy
flower-killing moon

April first
all but the fools
stay home

quarantine movie night
this urge to warn the actors
"keep your distance!"

my choice of fabric
for a pandemic mask . . .
the Deathly Hallows

face to face . . .
behind the mask
I stick out my tongue

my efforts
to flatten the curve . . .
distant thunder

keeping my distance
. . . the shadows of birds
touch

news of killer bees
and murder hornets . . .
the dragon moon

pandemic
the echinacea blooms
anyway

heavy rain
the steady pour
of vodka

TANKA

as a mother
I know your heart
in the way
elephants speak
through the ground

wrapped
in an old woman's skin
spring moon
do you know
what I know?

as are moths
I am free to fly
yet I turn
in this endless circle
around your artificial light

a fly
crawling on its side
breaks loose
this flood of memories
my father in his last hours

wind
drives the high clouds
into one another
from below I study
the motionless bits of blue

no makeup
no adornments
and yet
some things remain
hidden from view

HAIBUN

Emily

She pulled up to class on her bicycle. As confident as any precocious eleven-year-old, she kicked the stand down and pulled off her helmet. Once inside, Emily greeted the adults in the drawing class with sneers and complained, "My mother followed me in the car. She always promises she won't, but she does." Amid a few chuckles, she stormed to her chair and deposited her drawing pad and pencils. "She lies. It's really just lying!"

The only child in an adult drawing class, Emily has the hearts of everyone in the room.

"It's what parents do," I assured her, "wanting to watch out for their children."

Brenda leaned in and said, "You will appreciate your mother's concern when you are older and have kids of your own."

Everyone tried to calm her frustration, but Emily would not be placated. "I tell her not to follow me, but she always does."

We watched her mood soften as she concentrated on that evening's assignment. Each of us remembered our childhood struggles, but we are also parents. At the end of class we assured her, again, that mothers and fathers only smother us because they care. With a scowl, she climbed on her bike and rode away.

Today a friend asked if I had heard.

"Heard what?"

Emily had been struck by a car while riding her bike home from our art class. Her leg was fractured.

fledglings . . .
a baby praying mantis
on her finger

Letting Go

There was an element of play-
fulness missing from my 34-year
marriage. My ex is a good man,
and was kind to me throughout
our time together, but he is
impatient and far too serious. In
the three years since our divorce,
I've learned to let my hair down.

      retired couple
      she breaks away to walk
      through a leaf pile

Another Round

The bartender rants about his
sister-in-law—*the gold digger*—
and how she manipulated his
brother into bed, into marriage.
This bartender who lives in his
brother's basement.

mockingbird
black and white feathers
in a gray forest

For Gene

We spent more than a few nights harassing each other via the Internet—he, teasing about his virility; and me, feigning embarrassment. We talked of addictions, of disappointments. Of weariness. He offered to fly halfway across the country to see if we could make a go of it. I balked at entering what could only be a doomed relationship.

"I would be the perfect house husband," he said, "attending your every desire."

"You would overwhelm me," I told him, fearing the suffocating need inherent in his words.

the child he lost—
the child he has become

"Lost In Translation"

Exploring Japanese Short-form Poetry

Did you know that haiku is:

- *composed of two parts*
- *must include a "link and shift"*
- *should be present tense*
- *should not tell the reader what to think*
- *can be funny*
- *has a hundred (sometimes conflicting) rules*

The word "haiku" is both singular and plural, and the poetry genre has its origins in social poetry called renku. Many schools use haiku as a teaching tool for children, but it is far from an elementary form of literature. For centuries, it has been practiced by Japanese royalty and the elite.

When linguists from the West first came in contact with the Japanese language, they missed a few things in their translations. For one, Japanese sound units do not correlate to English syllables. And Western culture was not familiar with the tradition of placing haiku in the season it was written, requiring that a "kigo" be included in the poem.

Following are a few basic things to consider when reading and, perhaps, writing traditional haiku:

Phrase and fragment—

Most often, haiku are composed of two parts —a <u>phrase</u> and a <u>fragment</u>. They are usually incomplete sentences and frequently sound unfinished. Try to <u>avoid intentional rhymes</u>. Avoid capitals or punctuation when possible. This leaves a sense of openness for the reader to explore. <u>Don't get fancy.</u>

Link and shift—

The haiku should create a <u>link</u> between the two parts and yet contain a subtle <u>shift</u> that opens the poem to something new. Look for the *aha* moment. If the link is too strong, the poem may fall flat. Conversely, if it is too subtle, the reader may get lost.

Present tense—

Haiku should be written in the present tense. Imagine the reader standing where you are and experiencing exactly the same thing you experience <u>in that very moment</u>.

Be concrete—

Tell the reader about something they can <u>see</u>, <u>hear</u>, <u>touch</u>, <u>taste</u>, <u>smell</u>. It is best to include only those things you can prove. You may also tell the reader what you personally are feeling/thinking, but not what others are feeling/thinking.

Don't tell the reader what to think—

<u>Keep opinions to yourself</u>. The rose may be "beautiful" to you but not to the next person. Western poetry often leaves little room for maneuvering. Japanese short–form poetry puts a great deal of trust in the reader to bring his/her own experience to the poem.

Eliminate unnecessary adjectives—

Is it important that your reader knows if the ball is red or the pillow is soft? If not, <u>leave it out</u>. Haiku is so short that filling it up with unnecessary adjectives leaves little room for getting your point across.

what do I see . . .

what do I hear . . .

what do I smell . . .

what do I taste . . .

what do I touch . . .

what are my thoughts . . .